International Praise for ... DEVELOPING **HIGH PERFORMANCE TEAMS**

"This book is a must read. Walt Natemeyer understands the power of successful people, teams and organizations. His insight, gained over years of working with and observing the best and brightest, is well worth any leader's time."

—John Duncan
HR Manager, Apache Energy Ltd, Australia

"This book offers invaluable advice on how to build high performance teams. I have used Walt's techniques for many years, and I strongly recommend them to leaders at all levels."

—Cyril Odu
Vice Chairman and CFO, Mobil Producing Nigeria,
ExxonMobil Corporation

"Since I first attended a seminar with Walt Natemeyer in Bogotá in 1999, I have been a believer in what an effective team can do for an organization. To build a high performance team you need to follow a process that emphasizes trust, care, understanding, continuous development and taking advantage of every team member's strengths. Walt Natemeyer was the first to teach me these things and what I learned has helped me create highly effective teams in our organization."

—Carlos Sarmiento
General Manager, Schlumberger Ecuador

"*Developing High Performance Teams* is filled with clear, practical guidelines for clarifying the future direction of teams and developing action plans to improve. I have worked with Walt Natemeyer in locations around the world. His techniques consistently lead to significantly increased team and organizational effectiveness."

—Mark R. Ward
Chairman and Managing Director, Mobil Producing Nigeria,
ExxonMobil Corporation

To Jason -
With Best Wishes -

DEVELOPING HIGH PERFORMANCE TEAMS

SECOND EDITION

Walter E. Natemeyer, Ph.D.

North American Training and Development, Inc.

April 2012

For more than fifty years, human space exploration has thrilled us with spectacular accomplishments and reminded us of its inherent risks. There is no work environment more challenging and unforgiving than outer space.

High Performance Teams are essential to minimize risks and accomplish difficult missions in perilous, complicated, and technologically challenging situations. As you face challenges in your business, join us on this journey to develop High Performance Teams.

STS-95 Onboard View. The seven crew members pose for their traditional in-flight crew portrait October 29, 1998.

Photo courtesy of NASA, Johnson Space Center, Houston, Texas.

DEVELOPING HIGH PERFORMANCE TEAMS

SECOND EDITION

Walter E. Natemeyer, Ph.D.
North American Training and Development, Inc.

NATD Publications is a Division of North American Training and Development, Inc.

This is the International Space Station photographed soon after the space shuttle Atlantis and the station began their post-undocking separation on November 25, 2009.
Photo courtesy of NASA

This book celebrates the International Space Station (ISS), which is an internationally-developed research facility that holds the current record for the longest uninterrupted human presence in space. Construction of the ISS began in 1998 and was completed in 2011. The International Space Station is expected to remain in operation until 2020.

The ISS is operated as a joint project between five participating space agencies:

- National Aeronautics and Space Administration (NASA) USA
- European Space Agency (ESA)
- Russian Federal Space Agency (RKA)
- Japan Aerospace Exploration Agency (JAXA)
- Canadian Space Agency (CSA)

The International Space Station Program was nominated for the *Nobel Peace Prize* in 2010. It is an extraordinary example of how a positive and inspiring goal can align people from many nations and build cooperation, trust, and mutual respect among all team members.

DEVELOPING HIGH PERFORMANCE TEAMS

SECOND EDITION

Library of Congress Control Number: 2011910221

For more information, contact:
NATD Publications
17041 El Camino Real, Suite 103
Houston, Texas 77058-2668 USA
Phone (281) 488-7000
Fax (281) 488-7088
www.natraining.com

Printed in the United States of America

To my Parents

Paula and Ernst Natemeyer

Who taught me the importance of

dedication to work and

sensitivity to others

TABLE OF CONTENTS

PREFACE

Developing High Performance Teams is a compilation of team building and strategic planning activities aimed at dramatically increasing team effectiveness. North American Training and Development, Inc. has developed and refined these techniques working with more than 100 organizations over the past 35 years. One of the most gratifying aspects of our work has been the opportunity to observe the increased vitality, performance, and satisfaction that result from evolving into a "High Performance Team."

ABOUT THE AUTHOR

Dr. Walter E. Natemeyer is the CEO of North American Training and Development, Inc. He received his BBA and MBA from Ohio University and his Ph.D. in organizational behavior from the University of Houston. Dr. Natemeyer was a professor of management and organizational behavior at Ohio University and the University of Houston. He currently teaches in the EMBA Program at the University of Chicago.

Also, he served for five years as Director of the NASA Johnson Space Center Management Development Program. He has designed and conducted leadership and team development programs for more than 100 major organizations in the United States and abroad.

Dr. Natemeyer lives with his wife Mona on Galveston Bay near Houston, Texas. They have three children and four grandchildren.

Together

Everyone

Achieves

More

CHAPTER 1

— INTRODUCTION —

Astronauts work together on the final of three space walks of the first ISS assembly mission.

Photo courtesy of NASA

INTRODUCTION

Organizations worldwide have recognized the importance of teams to success in today's increasingly competitive and fast-paced business environment. The popularity of the "team concept" has created a heightened concern for functioning effectively as a team to maximize the payoff from teamwork. Teams of all kinds and configurations are engaging in "Team Building" activities to become more focused, more innovative and more productive.

This book is intended to serve as a guide to becoming a "High Performance Team." The techniques described are based on the team building work we have done in more than 100 business and governmental organizations since 1975. I encourage you to explore "Team Building Techniques" with us, and more importantly, to apply these activities within your organization. The journey to team excellence is exciting, fun and worth the trip. Isn't it time for you and your teammates to get started?

TEAMS IN ORGANIZATIONS

People have always worked in groups to perform tasks that could not be accomplished by one person. Organizations are comprised of many groups of varying size, composition, duration, and purpose. Not all of these groups are teams. What distinguishes a "team" from a group is an ongoing commitment by the team members to place the common goal of the team above self-interest and to work together in a spirit of cooperation to get the job done.

A "TEAM" IS TWO OR MORE PEOPLE WORKING TOGETHER INTERDEPENDENTLY TO ACCOMPLISH A COMMON GOAL.

There are a multitude of groups within large, complex organizations. Employees and leaders are frequently members of numerous groups. Consider the types of groups that exist in organizations today.

Board of Directors
Executive Committee
Senior Management Team
Leadership Team
Department Team
Task Force Team
Safety Team
Quality Steering Committee
Reengineering Team
Long-Range Planning Team
Project Team
Breakthrough Team
Product Development Team
Sales Team
Multi-Disciplinary Team
Supplier-Customer Team
Labor-Management Team
Strategic Alliance Team
Continuous Improvement Team

Not all groups have the potential for becoming a team. Only those fitting the definition – working in a cooperative manner to accomplish a common goal – are likely to become high performance teams. Many organizations have tried to make all groups "teams" and failed because of the lack of the critical binding element – the common goal and the need for interdependent, cooperative action. Therefore, important questions to ask are:

- Is there a need for coordinated effort among our group members?
- What would be the benefits of evolving into a team?
- What would be the costs?
- What do we need to do to begin developing into a team?
- Should this group be a team?

When pondering these questions, most groups decide that becoming a "team" is desirable. As a result of this decision, "Team Building" activities have become commonplace in organizations throughout the world to enable groups to develop into teams.

What has caused the proliferation of teams within and, in many cases, between organizations? Quite simply, it is the realization that teams have tremendous potential to improve performance, innovation and overall effectiveness. Let's consider the potential advantages of working as a team.

POTENTIAL ADVANTAGES OF TEAMS

- ✔ Higher productivity
- ✔ Increased satisfaction of team members
- ✔ More innovation and creativity
- ✔ Better decisions
- ✔ Faster response time
- ✔ More commitment of team members
- ✔ Increased cooperation among team members
- ✔ More growth and development of team members

Unfortunately, all teams do not reap these benefits. In fact, some become vivid examples of the potential disadvantages – when time, money, and other resources are expended attempting to implement the team concept with little or no payoff.

McKinsey & Company consultants for Jon R. Katzenbach and Douglas K. Smith have studied teams for many years. Their best-selling book, *The Wisdom of Teams,* makes a compelling argument for why teams are a critical element in creating high performance organizations. Chapter 1 of *The Wisdom of Teams* is included in the Recommended Readings section of this book. It summarizes key lessons Katzenbach and Smith have learned about teams, why they are important to organizational performance, and how to overcome resistance in order to reap the benefits of developing high performance teams. Also included as Recommended Readings are excerpts from *The Performance Factor* by Pat MacMillan and *The Five Dysfunctions of a Team* by Patrick Lencioni.

The docked space shuttle Discovery and the Canadian-built Special Purpose Dextrous Manipulator (SPDM), are featured in this image photographed on February 26, 2011 by an STS-133 crew member on the International Space Station. The blackness of space and Earth's horizon provide the backdrop for the scene.

Photo courtesy of NASA, Johnson Space Center

TEAMWORK IS:

- THE ABILITY TO WORK TOGETHER TOWARD A COMMON VISION
- THE ABILITY TO DIRECT INDIVIDUAL ACCOMPLISHMENT TOWARD ORGANIZATIONAL OBJECTIVES
- THE FUEL THAT ALLOWS COMMON PEOPLE TO ATTAIN UNCOMMON RESULTS

THE TEAM BUILDING PROCESS

How can you successfully build a *High Performance Team*?

Team Building activities may provide the answer.

TEAM BUILDING:

THE PROCESS OF ASSESSING CURRENT TEAM EFFECTIVENESS, AND DEVELOPING AND IMPLEMENTING AN ACTION PLAN TO IMPROVE

Eight Key Steps in the Team Building Process:

1. ***Recognition that Team Building is Desirable***

2. ***Assessment of the Team's Effectiveness***

3. ***Discussion and Analysis of the Assessment Results***

4. ***Clarification of the Team's Vision, Mission, and Values***

5. ***Identifying the Team's Key Goals***

6. ***Development of the Team Action Plan***

7. ***Implementation of the Team Action Plan***

8. ***Action Plan Progress Review and Revision***

A discussion of each of these steps follows.

STEPS IN THE TEAM BUILDING PROCESS

1. *Recognition that Team Building is Desirable*

Team Building does not happen on its own. The process begins when someone within the organization or the team realizes that there are opportunities for improvement, and that devoting time and effort to "team building" activities is likely to lead to those improvements more quickly and successfully. To maximize the payoff from your team building activities, the team leaders must actively support the effort.

Their commitment should be demonstrated by their words and their deeds, i.e., personal involvement in the team building activities. Also, the leader should solicit support for the team and its improvement activities from his / her manager.

The more support and encouragement provided by the leaders, the more seriously team members will view the effort. Ultimately it is the recognition by the team members that team building is important and beneficial that will determine their involvement in and commitment to the process.

2. *Assessment of the Team's Effectiveness*

In order to determine where to focus your improvement efforts, the team's current effectiveness must be assessed. This information can be generated in a number of ways:

- One-on-one interviews with team members
- Open discussions with the team as a whole
- Structured surveys or questionnaires
- Input from members or leaders of other teams
- Input from customers or suppliers

These methods are discussed in greater detail later.

3. *Discussion and Analysis of the Assessment Results*

The data generated in Step 2 should be recorded, scored, processed, transcribed and reproduced for discussion and analysis by the entire team. This analysis serves as the basis for determining the team's strengths, weaknesses, opportunities, threats, key results areas, and key improvement areas.

4. *Clarification of the Team's Vision, Mission, and Values*

The team should then develop (or review and revise) its Mission Statement and goals for the next time period (usually a year). For some teams (i.e., a Senior Management Team), developing a "Vision Statement" and list of "Core Values" may also be desirable. The team's Vision, Mission, and Values serve as the basis for the Team Action Plan.

5. *Identifying the Team's Key Goals*

The team should then assess its current and future challenges, identify its "Key Results Areas," and select its "Key Improvement Areas" or goals.

6. *Development of the Team Action Plan*

Action items should be developed to achieve each of the team's goals. These action items should be designed to improve performance in each of the team's Key Improvement Areas. The action items must be **S**pecific, **M**easurable, **A**chievable, **R**elevant and **T**ime-bound (i.e., SMART). The responsibility for implementing the action (or leading the effort) and the time frame must be clearly defined.

7. *Implementation of the Team Action Plan*

Once finalized, the Team Action Plan needs to be implemented. Effort must be placed on getting started on the Action Plan promptly, monitoring progress on an on-going basis, acknowledging progress and addressing problems should they occur.

8. *Action Plan Progress Review and Revision*

A formal Action Plan Progress Review should be scheduled within three months. Each action item should be reviewed so that recognition can be given, progress can be assessed, and problems can be discussed and resolved. The Action Plan should then be revised in light of the progress that has been made and the changes that have occurred during the previous few months.

The Team Building Process is discussed in greater detail in the following three chapters:

CHAPTER 2

Planning the Team Building Session

CHAPTER 3

Conducting the Team Building Session

CHAPTER 4

Reviewing and Renewing Your Team Building Efforts

Expedition Three Cosmonaut flight engineers prepare the Russian Orlan space suit for an upcoming spacewalk from the Pirs Docking Compartment on the International Space Station (ISS), October 4, 2001.

Photo courtesy of NASA

CHAPTER 2

PLANNING THE TEAM BUILDING SESSION

We typically recommend a two-day Team Building Retreat. The session should be scheduled when all or most of the team leaders and members can be present, and when the team can focus its thoughts and attention on the Team Building process. Also, the location should be free of distractions. A skilled and experienced meeting facilitator should be selected to lead the Team Building session. This person should ideally be from outside the team and is often an external consultant. In any case, the facilitator should have a basic understanding of the organization's business and the team's role and responsibilities. Also, the meeting facilitator should have the support of the team leaders and be able to gain the trust of the team members quickly and effectively.

The pre-session activities should include:

- Checking schedules of the participants to ensure full or high attendance
- Selecting meeting dates, times, and location
- Informing participants of the objectives of the session
- Communicating the details of the agenda: including pre-workshop interview, workshop start and end times, location, arrangements for meals, transportation, lodging, etc.

Date: October 14, 2011

To: Team Member

Subject: TEAM BUILDING WORKSHOP
Scheduled for November 7-8, 2011

To help us progress toward becoming a High Performance Team, a two-day Team Building Workshop has been scheduled for November 7-8, 2011, at the Palace Hotel (1001 Main St., Houston TX).

The objectives for the workshop are as follows:

- To evaluate the effectiveness of our team
- To identify areas for improvement
- To increase awareness of team members' interpersonal styles
- To emphasize the need for more effective and open communication among team members
- To ensure focus on the team goals
- To develop a Team Action Plan and implementation strategy

This workshop will be facilitated by Dr. Walter E. Natemeyer of North American Training & Development, Inc. The two-day workshop begins on Monday, November 7, 2011 at 8:00 a.m. and ends between 5:00 and 6:00 p.m. We will then have a group dinner for workshop participants.

On Tuesday, the workshop will begin at 8:00 a.m. and will end no later than 4:00 p.m. Participants should make their own transportation arrangements to and from the workshop.

To prepare for the workshop and the pre-workshop interview with the consultant, please consider and write your response to this question:

> ***What are the key issues / concerns you would like to see addressed to increase the effectiveness of our team?***

Your response to this question will be the basis for a confidential discussion with the consultant on Thursday, November 3, 2011. (You may want to make a copy of your response for your records.)

Thank you in advance for your active participation in this important Team Building retreat. I look forward to working with you to increase our team's effectiveness.

Sincerely,

MRW
Team Leader

A very important pre-workshop activity is soliciting input from the participants regarding the key concerns that they would like to see addressed in the retreat. Many teams have not evolved to the point where everyone feels comfortable expressing their concerns openly and candidly. Therefore, conducting confidential one-on-one interviews with each team member provides an opportunity to identify what the team members would like to see changed in an effective and efficient manner.

The one-on-one interviews typically take 15 to 30 minutes. Each participant should be asked to consider the following question: "What are the key issues / concerns you would like to see addressed to increase the effectiveness of our team?" Having the participants write out their suggestions and bring two copies to the session can speed up the interview process. The interviewer should take the suggestions from each team member, paraphrase them into his / her own words and writing style, and review them with the team member to ensure that the suggestions have been accurately documented. (Using a laptop computer to record the comments as the participant speaks is a very effective method.)

Once the suggestions have been solicited from the team members, the interviewer should compile all of the information into one document to be reproduced and distributed to the participants during the session. Time permitting, the interviewer can organize the suggestions into different categories such as:

- Team goals and objectives
- Communication among team members
- Recognition and rewards for accomplishments
- Roles and responsibilities
- Team resources

The primary benefit of the pre-session interviews is that each team member's ideas are solicited in an anonymous manner and will be given some thought and attention during the team building session without fear of reprisal. Also, it will be very easy for the team to identify the key concerns of the team as a whole by reviewing all of the interview comments during the retreat and determining how many times the same issue is mentioned. We have consistently observed that these interviews allow the team to identify and address important issues quickly and effectively.

TEAMWORK

TALENT WINS GAMES, BUT TEAMWORK AND INTELLIGENCE WIN CHAMPIONSHIPS.

MICHAEL JORDAN, NBA SUPERSTAR

CHAPTER 3

CONDUCTING THE TEAM BUILDING SESSION

The Team Building Retreat is an important opportunity for the work group to develop into a team. Asking for everyone's active involvement and a positive attitude is an excellent way for the facilitator or team leader to kick things off.

A typical agenda for a two-day retreat is as follows:

PEOPLE DIFFER NOT ONLY IN THEIR ABILITY TO DO BUT ALSO IN THEIR "WILL TO DO."

THE TEAM LEADER NEEDS TO USE THE APPROPRIATE LEADERSHIP STYLE WITH EACH TEAM MEMBER TO GET EVERYONE ON BOARD.

DR. PAUL HERSEY, CREATOR OF SITUATIONAL LEADERSHIP™

TEAM BUILDING AGENDA

DAY 1-

THE ESSENTIALS OF TEAM EFFECTIVENESS

I. **Overview and Objectives of Workshop**

II. **The Need for New "Paradigms"**

III. **Characteristics of Effective Teams**

IV. **Assessing the Effectiveness of Your Team**

A. The Team Effectiveness Survey

B. Suggestions for Increasing Your Team's Effectiveness

V. **Discussion of "Key Concerns" (Based on Interviews)**

VI. **Understanding Your Interpersonal Style**

VII. **What Can I Do To Help Others Do Their Jobs Better?**

TEAM BUILDING AGENDA

DAY 2-

INCREASING YOUR TEAM'S EFFECTIVENESS

I. Clarifying the Direction of Your Team

A. Clarifying Your Team's Vision, Mission, and Values

B. Conducting a "SWOT" Analysis

C. Identifying Your Key Results Areas

D. Selecting Your Key Improvement Areas

II. Developing Your Team Action Plan

III. Implementing Your Team Action Plan

IV. Planning Your Team Building Progress Review

V. Concluding Remarks

Each agenda item will now be described in more detail.

DAY 1-

THE ESSENTIALS OF TEAM EFFECTIVENESS

I. Overview and Objectives of Workshop

The Team Building session should begin with the facilitator welcoming the participants to the workshop, reviewing the objectives, and having the participants introduce themselves. The team leader should then state his / her goals for the retreat and encourage all team members to be active, positive, open and honest in discussing the team and how it can improve.

The leader should emphasize that Team Building is intended to be a constructive, not destructive, experience. Therefore it is important to have the courage and self-control to identify and address problems in a way that maintains an atmosphere of mutual respect. Thus, the focus should be on problems, not on people. Also, the leader should point out that anything that is said during the session will not be used against team members later. It is essential for any fear of reprisal to be eliminated.

II. The Need for New Paradigms

An excellent way to get the team thinking about change and communicating with each other is to discuss the concept of *paradigms.* Paradigms are sets of rules which prescribe a certain way of doing things. All of us develop paradigms which guide our behavior, and these paradigms exist in all aspects of our life, including our work, family, social and spiritual lives. The key point of the discussion is that our paradigms provide structure and direction in our lives – and that is good. However, if the world around us is changing – which it is – and we do not change our paradigms accordingly, we are certain to become less successful.

Joel A. Barker has written and lectured extensively on the topic of paradigms. Also, he has produced several excellent videos that describe how getting locked into old paradigms can limit the effectiveness of individuals, groups, organizations and countries. Viewing one of Barker's videos (such as *Discovering The Future – The Business of Paradigms*) can set the stage for a productive group discussion regarding the paradigms the participants perceive as blocking progress and that they would like to see changed in order to increase the effectiveness of the team. The paradigm shifts that are suggested should be recorded and used later in the session when the team assesses itself and formulates its action plan. An example of desired paradigm shifts is provided on the next page.

TEAM BUILDING WORKSHOP

PARADIGMS TO CHANGE

CURRENT PARADIGM	IMPROVED PARADIGM
One-way communication	Open communication (upward and downward)
Inadequate interaction among all team members	Regular interaction among all team members
Little or no feedback on performance	Positive feedback / rewards based on performance
Rigid work schedule	Flex-time schedule
No feedback from customers	Regularly solicit feedback from customers
Inadequate training	Provide appropriate training to increase team members' skills

III. Characteristics of Effective Teams

The next step is to identify characteristics of High Performance Teams. An excellent way to structure this discussion is to ask the participants to think of the best team and the worst team they have ever worked on and to list three to five key differences between those teams. The facilitator asks the team members to share their lists and compiles these "Team Excellence Factors" on a flip chart. The team list can then be used to validate another list of characteristics of effective teams that has been identified by other groups or research.

The research conducted by NATD over the past 35 years has identified ten key characteristics of High Performance Teams. These ten excellence factors were determined by comparing high-rated vs. low-rated teams (using several versions of the NATD Team Effectiveness Survey).

The key characteristics of highly effective teams are:

1. **Clear Direction** – Team members are clear on the team's Vision for the future and its Mission, goals and objectives.
2. **Appropriate Team Composition** – The team has the appropriate mix of knowledge, experience and skill, and it has effective leadership.
3. **Commitment to Roles and Responsibilities** – Roles and responsibilities are clearly and effectively defined, and team members take initiative to fulfill their assigned responsibilities.
4. **Effective Communication** – Team members communicate and cooperate well with each other, conduct effective meetings, and make good decisions.
5. **Adequate Resources** – The team has enough people, equipment, materials, information, and money to perform well.

6. **Focus on Quality and Customer Satisfaction** – The team measures quality and communicates effectively with customers to ensure that its products or services are "world-class."
7. **Innovation and Continuous Improvement** – Innovation and creativity are encouraged, mistakes are used as learning opportunities, and continuous improvement is a way of life on the team.
8. **Cooperation With Others** – The team communicates and cooperates well with other teams and responds quickly and effectively to requests.
9. **Appropriate Consequences** – Team members receive adequate feedback and recognition for their individual and team accomplishments, and performance problems are addressed and resolved quickly and effectively.
10. **Positive Results** – There is a high level of trust, respect, pride and enthusiasm on the team, and the team is highly productive and adds significant value to the organization.

After reviewing this or other lists of key excellence factors, the team members should be asked to think about how well they are functioning as a team.

IV. Assessing the Effectiveness of Your Team

After discussing the characteristics of high performance teams, the stage has been set for systematically assessing the team's effectiveness. We recommend using a structured questionnaire that will keep the discussion focused and provide baseline data which can be used to measure the team's progress in the future. There are many team effectiveness surveys available for this purpose. The one we use is based on the ten team excellence factors listed. The NATD Team Effectiveness Survey (TES) has two parts. Part 1 consists of fifty items which measure the ten characteristics of High Performance Teams. Part 2 is an open-ended question that solicits suggestions for increasing the team's effectiveness.

For your convenience, the copyrighted NATD *Team Effectiveness Survey* is reproduced here on the following pages. To purchase copies of this *Team Effectiveness Survey*, please contact the offices of North American Training and Development, Inc. by phone at 281-488-7000 or by email at wnatemeyer@natraining.com.

TEAM EFFECTIVENESS SURVEY

Developed by: Walter E. Natemeyer, PhD

____
Name of Team Member

INSTRUCTIONS:

This two-part survey provides you with the opportunity to respond to 50 items related to the team effectiveness of your work group (Part 1), and to make suggestions for improving team effectiveness (Part 2).

Part 1

Please read each statement carefully and consider the extent to which it describes your team. Indicate the extent of your agreement or disagreement by marking the appropriate response.

1 = Strongly Disagree
2 = Disagree
3 = Neutral
4 = Agree
5 = Strongly Agree

		Strongly Disagree	Disagree	Neutral	Agree	Strongly Agree
Clear Direction						
1.	Our team members share a clear and positive Vision of the future.	1	2	3	4	5
2.	Our team's Mission has been clearly defined.	1	2	3	4	5
3.	Team members are clear on our team's key results areas and goals.	1	2	3	4	5
4.	Our team's goals and objectives are clarified and updated on a regular basis.	1	2	3	4	5
5.	Our team's Mission and goals are aligned with those of the organization as a whole.	1	2	3	4	5
Appropriate Team Composition						
6.	We have the appropriate mix of knowledge and experience among our team members.	1	2	3	4	5
7.	Team members are highly skilled at what they do.	1	2	3	4	5
8.	Our team members have all the capability necessary to perform at a world-class level.	1	2	3	4	5
9.	Our team has adequate diversity of thought and opinion.	1	2	3	4	5
10.	Our team has highly effective leadership.	1	2	3	4	5

		Strongly Disagree	Disagree	Neutral	Agree	Strongly Agree
Commitment to Roles and Responsibilities						
11.	Roles and responsibilities are clearly defined within our team.	1	2	3	4	5
12.	Team members accept and buy into their assigned roles and responsibilities.	1	2	3	4	5
13.	Team members take initiative to fulfill their responsibilities.	1	2	3	4	5
14.	Someone is clearly responsible for all key tasks that our team is expected to do.	1	2	3	4	5
15.	The distribution of roles and responsibilities in our team allows work to be performed efficiently.	1	2	3	4	5
Effective Communication						
16.	Team members communicate openly and honestly with each other.	1	2	3	4	5
17.	Team members interact with each other frequently enough.	1	2	3	4	5
18.	Our team meetings are highly effective.	1	2	3	4	5
19.	Team members willingly and enthusiastically cooperate with each other.	1	2	3	4	5
20.	Our team makes decisions in a highly effective manner.	1	2	3	4	5
Adequate Resources						
21.	Our team has enough people to perform well.	1	2	3	4	5
22.	We are provided with the appropriate materials, tools and equipment to perform our assigned tasks.	1	2	3	4	5
23.	Our team has an adequate budget to enable us to perform well.	1	2	3	4	5
24.	Our team receives the information we need in an effective and timely manner.	1	2	3	4	5
25.	We receive a high level of support from other teams within our organization.	1	2	3	4	5
Focus on Quality and Customer Satisfaction						
26.	We regularly and systematically measure the quality of our team's products or services.	1	2	3	4	5
27.	Our team communicates effectively with our customers to solicit feedback about our performance.	1	2	3	4	5
28.	We are actively involved in "Bench Marking" activities to stay abreast of the "Best Practices" in our field.	1	2	3	4	5
29.	The products or services of our team are of world-class quality.	1	2	3	4	5
30.	Our team has built a strong, positive reputation as an effective and responsive team.	1	2	3	4	5

	Innovation and Continuous Improvement	Strongly Disagree	Disagree	Neutral	Agree	Strongly Agree
31.	Innovation and creativity are strongly encouraged within our team.	1	2	3	4	5
32.	Team members continuously develop and try out new ideas and techniques to improve what we do.	1	2	3	4	5
33.	Work processes are designed and reengineered as needed to ensure a high level of efficiency.	1	2	3	4	5
34.	Well-intentioned mistakes that result from reasonable risk-taking are viewed as learning opportunities.	1	2	3	4	5
35.	We are viewed by others as a highly creative and innovative team.	1	2	3	4	5
	Cooperation With Others					
36.	Our team communicates adequately with other teams or departments within our organization.	1	2	3	4	5
37.	Our team cooperates well with other teams or departments.	1	2	3	4	5
38.	We actively collaborate with other teams or departments on joint projects.	1	2	3	4	5
39.	We respond quickly and effectively to requests from other teams or departments.	1	2	3	4	5
40.	We are viewed as "Team Players" by others within our organization.	1	2	3	4	5
	Appropriate Consequences					
41.	Team members receive adequate feedback on their individual contributions.	1	2	3	4	5
42.	Individual accomplishments are adequately recognized and rewarded.	1	2	3	4	5
43.	We receive adequate feedback on our team performance.	1	2	3	4	5
44.	Team accomplishments are recognized and celebrated.	1	2	3	4	5
45.	Performance problems within our team are addressed and resolved quickly and effectively.	1	2	3	4	5
	Positive Results					
46.	Our team members respect each other.	1	2	3	4	5
47.	There is a high level of trust among team members.	1	2	3	4	5
48.	We have a high level of pride and enthusiasm on our team.	1	2	3	4	5
49.	We are a highly productive team that adds significant value to our organization.	1	2	3	4	5
50.	Overall, we are a highly effective team.	1	2	3	4	5

Please continue to Part 2 >>>

Part 2

In the space below please list your suggestions for increasing your team's effectiveness:

Address inquiries or orders to:

NORTH AMERICAN TRAINING AND DEVELOPMENT INC.
17041 El Camino Real, Suite 103
Houston, Texas 77058-2668
(281) 488-7000 • Fax (281) 488-7088
www.natraining.com

We recommend that each person individually rate the team's effectiveness and list suggestions for improvement. After that, the team should be divided into small groups of three to five people who will go back through the questionnaire item-by-item, share and discuss their individual ratings, and develop consensus ratings. The consensus ratings from each of the small groups should then be recorded and averaged. The data can be used to identify the team's strengths and weaknesses. Also, team members' suggestions for improvements should be discussed, and the group should select and record the ones that they consider the "Best Suggestions."

If possible, the data from Part 1 of the TES and a compilation of the "Best Suggestions" from Part 2 should immediately be reproduced and distributed to all team members. This information will not only be useful during subsequent activities in the workshop, but also as baseline data to measure the team's progress in the future. An example of "Key Concerns" from Part 1 and "Best Suggestions" from Part 2 is provided on the next page.

MARINE LOGISTICS TEAM BUILDING

November 7-8, 2011

TEAM EFFECTIVENESS SURVEY ANALYSIS

PART 1 – KEY CONCERNS (LOWEST SCORING ITEMS)

ITEM	AVG	CONCERNS
21	2.67	Our team has enough people to perform well
22	3.00	Our team has adequate materials to perform our tasks
23	3.00	Our team has an adequate budget
24	3.00	Our team receives the information we need
25	2.67	We receive support from other departments
42	3.33	Individuals' accomplishments are recognized and rewarded
44	3.33	Team accomplishments are recognized and celebrated
45	3.33	We address performance problems quickly and effectively

MARINE LOGISTICS TEAM BUILDING

November 7-8, 2011

TEAM EFFECTIVENESS SURVEY ANALYSIS

PART 2 – BEST SUGGESTIONS

TEAM 1

1. Communicate the need for more people, budget and equipment
2. Job descriptions, roles and responsibilities known to entire team
3. Formalized department meetings
4. Office enlargement / consolidation
5. Individual performance feedback

TEAM 2

1. Improve communication within the department
2. Define roles and responsibilities
3. Develop a high level of trust within the department
4. Reward accomplishments

V. Discussion of "Key Concerns" (Based on Interviews)

If interviews were conducted prior to the workshop, the team should then discuss the interview comments to further clarify the team members' key concerns. We recommend that a copy of all anonymous interview comments be distributed. In small groups, participants should read each comment out loud to ensure a clear understanding of all concerns on the minds of the team members. The groups should then develop a prioritized list of the key concerns expressed in these interview comments. The lists should be recorded on flip charts and shared with the entire team. An example is provided on the next page.

By this point in the workshop, the team will have systematically measured and discussed its effectiveness and identified the key concerns that participants would like to see addressed and resolved. The process we have described can be psychologically exhausting, but participants typically feel quite satisfied that their team's performance has been systematically and thoroughly assessed.

MARINE LOGISTICS TEAM BUILDING

November 7-8, 2011

TEAM EFFECTIVENESS INTERVIEW ANALYSIS

INTERVIEWS – KEY CONCERNS

TEAM 1

1. **Clarification:**
   - **organization chart**
   - **job descriptions**
   - **roles / responsibilities**
2. **Mid-year review**
3. **Prioritization of work**
4. **Communication (weekly meetings)**
5. **Safety indoctrination**

TEAM 2

1. **Improve communication (internal and external)**
2. **One location for entire team**
3. **Clarify roles and responsibilities**
4. **Improve customer buy-in**
5. **Mid-year review**

MARINE LOGISTICS TEAM BUILDING

November 7-8, 2011

TEAM EFFECTIVENESS INTERVIEW ANALYSIS

INTERVIEWS - KEY CONCERNS (CONSENSUS)

1. **Clarify roles and responsibilities**
2. **Improve communication**

   A. Internal

   B. External
3. **Periodic performance reviews**
4. **Safety training**
5. **Work prioritization**

STAGES OF TEAM DEVELOPMENT

In order for a team to analyze its current situation, it can be helpful to review typical stages of team development and to assess where it is as a team. This discussion can help team members understand why certain issues are critical at the present time and what their priorities should be to facilitate further development.

TEAMWORK

THE MOST EFFECTIVE LEADERS NEVER SAY "I". THEY THINK "WE". THEY THINK "TEAM".

THEY UNDERSTAND THAT THEIR JOB IS TO MAKE THE TEAM FUNCTION EFFECTIVELY.

PETER DRUCKER, MANAGEMENT AUTHOR

Many models have been developed to explain how teams evolve. The most popular was developed by Bruce W. Tuckman.[1] He suggests that a team goes through four distinct stages as it matures into a high performance team. The four stages are:

Forming This initial stage is marked by uncertainty and even confusion. Team members are usually highly motivated, but they are unsure about the team's purpose, structure and goals.

Storming This stage is characterized by conflict and confrontation as the team strives to clarify its structure, goals and roles.

Norming In this stage team members begin to settle into patterns of cooperation and collaboration. They are evolving into a "Team" characterized by high cohesion and a sense of team identity.

Performing At this stage the team has evolved into a High Performance Team that is highly committed to accomplishing its goals through collaborative effort.

[1] Bruce W. Tuckman, "Developmental Sequence in Small Groups," Psychological Bulletin, Nov. 1965: 384-399.

In a subsequent article, Tuckman and Jensen[2] point out that the fifth **"Adjourning"** stage may also occur. At this stage the team disbands because its goals have been accomplished, the team's responsibilities have been transferred to another team (within or outside the organization), or the team's activities are no longer needed.

In assessing where a team is in its development, team members will often decide that they are at more than one stage. For instance, for work that has been performed for an extended period of time, they may be at the Performing stage, but for a new project that has been assigned to them, they may be Forming or Storming. After analyzing the team's current stage, team members should discuss the appropriate actions they should take to move the team forward. These potential actions should be recorded for use in the Team Action Planning Process later in the Team Building Session.

[2] Bruce W. Tuckman and Mary Ann C. Jensen, "Stages of Small-Group Development Revisited," Group and Organization Studies, Dec. 1977: 419-427.

For instance, at the **Forming** stage, high priority actions typically include:

- Clarify the Purpose of the Team
  [Vision, Mission, Values, etc.]
- Clarify the Team's Structure and Composition
- Clarify Individual Roles and Responsibilities
- Identify Behaviors Expected of Team Members / Leaders
- Establish Meeting Rules

At the **Storming** stage, high-priority actions typically include:

- Identify Key Issues, Concerns, and Disagreements
- Analyze the Cause and Effect of These Issues, Concerns, and Disagreements
- Clarify the Team's Current Priorities
- Ensure Team is Moving in the Appropriate Direction
- Formulate a Team Action Plan to Address Key Issues / Concerns

At the **Norming** stage, high priority actions typically include:

- Assess Team Progress and Performance
- Ensure Alignment of all Team Members' Activities Toward Accomplishing the Team Mission
- Identify and Address Any Unresolved Issues or Concerns
- Identify Additional Opportunities for Collaborative Efforts

- Reaffirm Team Members' Commitment to their Individual Roles and Responsibilities
- Review/Revise Team Mission, Charter, and Action Plan

At the **Performing** stage, high priority actions typically include:

- Review Progress with Input from All Team Members and Key Stakeholders
- Recognize Individual Accomplishments
- Identify Ways for Individuals and the Team to Improve
- Periodically Update the Team's Mission, Goals, and Action Plan
- Celebrate Team Progress and Success

At the **Adjourning** stage, high priority actions typically include:

- Plan the Orderly Termination of the Team
- Make Sure All Documentation is Completed, Organized, and Accessible
- Capture "Lessons Learned"
- Communicate Necessary Information and Lessons Learned to all Appropriate People, Groups, and Organizations
- Provide Appropriate Recognition for Individual and Team Accomplishments

We will now shift our focus from the team to the individual team members.

VI. Understanding Your Interpersonal Style

Teams are made up of individuals who vary considerably in their personal, educational and work-life experiences. Also, there will undoubtedly be differences in their values, needs and interpersonal styles. For teams to function effectively, team members must learn to understand and accept the unique characteristics of each person and view this diversity as a team strength. If the team can build on each person's strengths and strive to help each other overcome weaknesses, everyone will benefit and the team will become stronger and more effective.

Discussing individual team member's characteristics and behavior can be a delicate matter - particularly for people who lack self-confidence, are highly sensitive, or are very private or shy. However, if the discussion is facilitated in a skillful manner, the team is likely to grow significantly in its understanding, valuing and acceptance of each team member.

To provide a forum for discussing individual characteristics or traits, team building programs often include an interpersonal style questionnaire. There are literally hundreds of these surveys available. Three of the most popular profiles will now be described.

The Myers - Briggs Type Indicator

The Myers - Briggs Type Indicator is the most widely used personality profile in the world. It measures individual preferences on four scales:

Extroverting	vs.	Introverting
Sensing	vs.	Intuiting
Thinking	vs.	Feeling
Judging	vs.	Perceiving

Based on your responses to the survey, you will receive a score that classifies you as follows:

E (Extroverting)	or	**I**	(Introverting)
S (Sensing)	or	**N**	(Intuiting)
T (Thinking)	or	**F**	(Feeling)
J (Judging)	or	**P**	(Perceiving)

E	indicates that you prefer to focus on the outer world of people and things, getting your energy from them
I	indicates that you prefer to focus on the inner world of ideas and impressions, getting your energy from them
S	indicates that you tend to focus on the present and on concrete information gained from your senses
N	indicates that you tend to focus on the future, with a view toward patterns and possibilities
T	indicates that you tend to base your decisions on logic and on objective analysis of cause and effect
F	indicates that you tend to base your decisions on values and on subjective evaluation of person-centered concerns
J	indicates that you like a planned and organized approach to life and prefer to have things settled
P	indicates that you like a flexible and spontaneous approach to life and prefer to keep your options open

There are sixteen different personality types (such as "ESTJ"), and each one is described in the survey report form. A key point from this exercise is that we should strive to understand and accept the unique characteristics of ourselves and others, and use this knowledge to communicate effectively.

The Myers - Briggs Type Indicator is available to qualified facilitators from Consulting Psychologists Press (CPP) at 1-800-624-1765 or www.cpp.com.

The Social Style Inventory

The Social Style profile measures two dimensions of interpersonal behavior:

Assertiveness – the degree to which a person's behavior is forceful and directive

Responsiveness – the degree to which a person's behavior is emotionally responsive and expressive

Depending on your scores, you will be classified into one of four Social Styles.

Driver	• High assertiveness and low responsiveness
Expressive	• High assertiveness and high responsiveness
Amiable	• Low assertiveness and high responsiveness
Analytical	• Low assertiveness and low responsiveness

Drivers are independent, candid, decisive, pragmatic and efficient.

Expressives are outgoing, enthusiastic, persuasive, fun-loving and spontaneous.

Amiables are cooperative, supportive, diplomatic, patient and loyal.

Analyticals are logical, thorough, serious, systematic and prudent.

This survey provides a great deal of information about the behavior of team members, as well as helpful information on how to communicate effectively with each of the four personality types.

Information about the Social Style Inventory is available from the TRACOM Group at 1-800-221-2321 or at www.tracom.com.

The Personal Profile

The Personal Profile measures four aspects of interpersonal style:

Dominance	• How much you try to control or dominate people and events
Influence	• How much you attempt to influence others through friendly persuasion
Steadiness	• How much you prefer stable, predictable situations and relationships
Conscientiousness	• How much you value precision, accuracy and attention to detail

Depending on your highest scoring category, you are classified as a **D, I, S** or **C** personality. Typical behaviors of these four primary styles are as follows:

D's want to be in control, have a strong ego and positive self-concept, are impatient, enjoy variety / change, and want the "bottom line" - not all the details.

I's are people-oriented, animated and expressive, often disorganized, thrive on social approval and are optimistic.

S's are steady and controlled, loyal and possessive, family-oriented, desire security, and do not like abrupt change.

C's are perfectionists, accurate, very attentive to detail, sensitive (especially about their work) and want extensive explanations.

The Personal Profile provides a wealth of information about the interpersonal styles of all team members and suggests ways to interact more effectively with each of the four styles. The Personal Profile is available to certified facilitators from Inscape Publishing 1-800-653-3472 or at www.inscapepublishing.com.

The key point of these and other interpersonal style exercises is that team and personal effectiveness will be enhanced if team members increase their understanding of themselves and the basic personalities of their colleagues. This will help team members interpret behavior and communicate with others in a more open, constructive and effective manner.

As Joe Luft and Harry Ingham have suggested in the *Johari Window*, the more people solicit feedback from others and openly disclose information to others, the greater the potential for effective interpersonal behavior. These profiles can help teams develop a more productive "arena" based on openness, acceptance and trust.

VII. What Can I Do To Help Others Do Their Jobs Better?

The final agenda item for Day 1 is a personal feedback session to increase each team member's awareness of what they can do to help others do their jobs better and to increase the effectiveness of the team. One at a time, team members are sent out of the meeting room. The remaining members develop a list of three to five "Strengths" that this person brings to the team, and three to five "Suggestions" for this person to help others do their jobs better and increase team effectiveness. The strengths and suggestions should be developed in an atmosphere of cooperation and mutual respect. When the lists for person one are finished, person two should be assessed (person two leaves the room and sends in person one), and then person three, and so on.

After all team members have been assessed, they should be de-briefed on their strengths and suggestions lists. We suggest that participants listen to their feedback with an open mind, refrain from responding defensively, and focus on what they can do to improve their contributions to the team.

If the team members develop these lists and provide the feedback in a positive, non-emotional manner, and the information is accepted in good faith, the team will have taken a giant step toward creating an environment where constructive suggestions are provided and accepted on an on-going basis. This feedback is essential to the continual growth and development of all team members.

We suggest that the team leader encourage team members to implement the suggestions for improvement they receive, and to indicate that the lists will be reviewed in a follow-up session to assess each person's progress on becoming a more effective team member.

VISION

NOTHING HAPPENS
UNLESS FIRST A DREAM.

CARL SANDBURG, POET

President John F. Kennedy addressed a joint session of Congress May 25, 1961 stating:

"I believe that this nation should commit itself to achieving the goal, before this decade is out, of landing a man on the moon and returning him safely to the Earth."

—Photo courtesy of NASA

DAY 2-

INCREASING YOUR TEAM'S EFFECTIVENESS

During the second day of the program, the team will go through a systematic process to clarify the direction of the team, assess its current and future environment, and decide what it must do well and what it must improve.

These discussions serve as the basis for developing a detailed Action Plan to increase team effectiveness. These "Strategic Planning" activities are essential ingredients in motivating teams to take the initiative to face up to their challenges and take bold steps to improve.

At the beginning of this exercise, it is desirable to briefly review the overall organization's Vision, Mission, and Values. This will help participants align their team's Mission and goals with those of the organization as a whole.

Reviewing Your Organization's Vision

A Vision is a statement of what the organization intends to be or do in the future.

Ford (Early 1900s)	• Democratize the automobile
Stanford (1940s)	• Become the Harvard of the West
Boeing (1950s)	• Become the dominant player in commercial aircraft and bring the world into the jet age
McDonald's (1960s)	• Be the world's best quick service restaurant
General Electric (1980s)	• Become number one or number two in every market we serve
Toyota (1980s)	• Become the biggest and best automobile maker in the world
Amazon (2000s)	• Be the world's most customer-centric company; to build a place online where people can come to find and discover anything they might want to buy
Google (2010s)	• Organize the world's information and make it universally accessible and useful

Reviewing Your Organization's Mission

A Mission is a statement of what you are in business to do (i.e., your organization's reason for being).

ExxonMobil	• ExxonMobil Corporation is committed to being the world's premier petroleum and petrochemical company. To that end, we must continuously achieve superior financial and operating results while adhering to the highest standards of business conduct. These unwavering expectations provide the foundation for our commitments to those with whom we interact.
Hewlett-Packard	• To make technical contributions for the advancement and welfare of humanity
3M	• To solve unsolved problems innovatively
Hewlett-Packard	• To make technical contributions for the advancement and welfare of humanity
Merck	• To preserve and improve human life
The Walt Disney Company	• To make people happy

Reviewing Your Organization's Values

Your Values are the strongly-held beliefs and principles that guide your organization's strategies and decisions on a daily basis.

A List of Commonly Cited Values:

- Total Commitment to Safety and the Environment
- Unwavering Dedication to Customer Satisfaction
- Honesty, Integrity, and Ethical Business Practices
- Genuine Concern for Our Employees and Their Families
- Open and Effective Communication
- Continuous Improvement in All Areas of Our Business

Apache Corporation's Core Values:

- Conduct Business with Honesty and Integrity
- Respect and Invest in Our Greatest Asset: Our People
- Conduct Business with Respect for People, Cultures, and Traditions
- Foster an Entrepreneurial Spirit, and Expect and Reward Innovation and Creativity
- Drive to Succeed with a Sense of Urgency

ExxonMobil Corporation's Core Values:

The following principles guide our relationships with our shareholders, customers, employees, and communities:

- ***Shareholders*** - We are committed to enhancing the long-term value of the investment dollars entrusted to us by our shareholders. By running the business profitably and responsibly, we expect our shareholders to be rewarded with superior returns. This commitment drives the management of our corporation.
- ***Customers*** - Success depends on our ability to consistently satisfy ever-changing customer preferences. We commit to being innovative and responsive, while offering high-quality products and services at competitive prices.
- ***Employees*** - The exceptional quality of our workforce provides a valuable competitive edge. To build on this advantage, we will strive to hire and retain the most qualified people available and to maximize their opportunities for success through training and development. We are committed to maintaining a safe work environment, enriched by diversity, and characterized by open communication, trust, and fair treatment.
- ***Communities*** - We commit to be a good corporate citizen in all the places we operate worldwide. We will maintain high ethical standards, obey all applicable laws, rules, and regulations, and respect local and national cultures. Above all other objectives, we are dedicated to running safe and environmentally responsible operations.

NASA's Core Values:

Mission success requires uncompromising commitment to:

- Safety
- Excellence
- Teamwork
- Integrity

Schlumberger's Guiding Principles for Values, Conduct, and Behavior:

Making the most of our unique assets, Schlumberger is committed to providing services that enhance and optimize our customers' performance.

Three well-established company Values that focus on people, technology, and profit serve as the basis for our work:

- Our people thrive on the challenge to excel in any environment, and their dedication to safety and customer service worldwide is our greatest strength.
- Our commitment to technology and quality is the basis for our competitive advantage.
- Our determination to produce superior profits is the cornerstone for our future independence of action and growth.

I. Clarifying the Direction of Your Team

A. Clarifying Your Team's Mission

After reviewing the organization's Vision, Mission, and Values, the next step is to define (or to review and revise) the team's "Mission Statement." The "Mission" should be a statement of what the team is in business to do to support the organization's overall Vision, Mission, Values, and Goals. To stimulate thought and discussion, a good question to ask is, "What are we being paid by our organization to do?"

The Mission statement should be 25 words or less and be clearly and concisely worded. It should be a Mission that:

- all team members agree with and enthusiastically support
- a new team member can understand
- aligns with the organization's Vision, Mission, Values, and Goals
- will be approved and supported by top management

A clear and concise Mission statement can be very useful in providing the team with a common purpose, aligning the team members in that direction, and keeping them focused on an on-going basis. While some dispute the value of developing Mission statements, we find that it is an essential step in the team building process. If developed quickly and effectively, virtually all team members will view the process as time well spent.

B. Conducting a SWOT" Analysis

The second step is to conduct a SWOT Analysis (Strengths, Weaknesses, Opportunities, Threats), which consists of assessing and listing your current strengths and current weaknesses, and thinking ahead to analyze and list your future opportunities and future threats.

Strengths

When the team assessed its effectiveness on Day 1 (using a Team Effectiveness Survey), it identified its strengths and weaknesses as a team. Using the data from the survey (in particular the highest scoring items), and a more subjective discussion of the clear strengths that the team possesses, participants should develop a list of the team's current strengths. In our day-to-day work life, as well as in team building sessions like this, there is a tendency to focus on the negative, on what is wrong rather than what is right. The team should take some time to acknowledge and utilize its positive attributes, and this discussion gives the team an opportunity to do that.

Weaknesses

The team can also use the data from the Team Effectiveness Survey (in this case the lowest scoring items), the interview comments and analysis, and the overall discussion on Day 1 to identify and list its current weaknesses. If a team is going to succeed at increasing its effectiveness, it must have the courage to admit its shortcomings. During this discussion, it can be helpful if the leader encourages the team to be candid and reminds them that if they do not recognize and acknowledge problems, they will be unlikely to do anything to improve. These weaknesses will be used as a basis for selecting key improvement areas and action items later in the day.

Opportunities

In addition to assessing the current situation in determining what and how to improve, we believe that teams should also focus on anticipating the future, and planning to seize opportunities before others in order to gain a competitive advantage. In this analysis, the team members should strive to think "outside the box" and consider future opportunities that could benefit the team and the organization during the next three to five years. In developing this list, the team should also begin to discuss what it can do to increase the probability that these circumstances will materialize as well as what it should do to maximize the payoff from seizing these opportunities.

Threats

The team should also be concerned about future threats that could devastate the team and/or the overall organization. In this discussion the participants should thoroughly consider negative scenarios that could unfold in the future. By anticipating the worst, the team is likely to be in a better position to take steps to reduce the probability that the worst will occur, and be in a stronger position to minimize the damage should those negative circumstances materialize.

C. Identifying Your Key Results Areas

The next step is to determine the team's Key Results Areas (KRAs).

These Key Results Areas, which are also called "critical success factors," are ***the most important things the team must do well in order to achieve its Mission***. It is best to limit this list to four to six KRAs, and to minimize the number of words used to describe the KRA (two to five words is best). After determining its KRAs, the team should list them in a prioritized order.

KRA lists typically include items related to:

- Performance / Productivity
- Cost Effectiveness
- Quality
- Innovation
- Marketing
- Customer Service
- Communication
- Compliance (i.e., Health, Safety, Environment, etc.)

D. Selecting Your Key Improvement Areas

The final step before developing the team's Action Plan is to determine its Key Improvement Areas (KIAs). Teams will often develop action plans based on their Key Results Areas. We prefer to take the selection process one step further and ask the team to consider everything that has been discussed in the past two days including:

- Paradigms to Change
- Team Effectiveness Survey Results and Suggestions for Improvement
- Interview Comments and Key Concerns
- Mission Statement
- SWOT Analysis
- Key Results Areas

With all of that information in mind, what are the most important areas in which the team must improve in order to significantly increase its effectiveness? In some cases, the KRA list and the KIA list will be identical. However, if the group feels that it is already performing well on some of its KRAs and that generating ideas on how to improve in these areas will add little value, there will be different items on the KIA list.

In selecting their KIAs, the team members should focus on the three to five areas where they need to improve significantly in order to successfully achieve their Mission. These KIAs should be prioritized and listed. They will serve as the basis of the Team Action Plan.

An example of a team's Mission, "SWOT" Analysis, Key Results Areas and Key Improvement Areas is provided on the following pages.

MARINE LOGISTICS TEAM BUILDING

November 7-8, 2011

MISSION STATEMENT

To provide and maintain safe, continuous and efficient marine service to our customers while optimizing vessel requirements.

STRENGTHS

1. Flexibility
2. Experience
3. Progressive management
4. Efficient service to our customers

WEAKNESSES

1. Inadequate headcount
2. Weak security at jetty
3. Lack of job descriptions
4. Old vessels
5. Inadequate communication

OPPORTUNITIES

1. Scheduled service
2. Fleet reduction
3. Improved communication with customers
4. Build harbor

MARINE LOGISTICS TEAM BUILDING

November 7-8, 2011

THREATS

1. Low Funding
2. Increased Use of Low-Performing Contractors
3. No Hiring
4. Outsourcing

KEY RESULTS AREAS

1. Safety, Reliability and Deliverability
2. Service Measurement and Responsiveness
3. Effective Prioritization
4. Flexibility

KEY IMPROVEMENT AREAS

1. Improve Communication
    - Internal (including clarifying roles and responsibilities)
    - External (including measurement of customer service)
2. Obtain Approval for Harbor
3. Institute Scheduled Sailings
4. Increase Funding

E. Clarifying Roles and Responsibilities

The need to clarify Team Member's roles and responsibilities is an on-going process because of ever-changing business objectives. It is especially critical when a new team is formed, a new Team Leader / Manager comes into the group, or an organization restructures. For the team to function effectively and to ensure that existing and new objectives will be achieved, the following exercise can make a significant difference.

After the team has clarified its Mission, each member should write his / her role in the team on a flip chart page. Rather than merely writing down the person's job title (Construction Manager, Superintendent, Transport Coordinator, Project Engineer, etc.), it is important to completely describe the person's function on the team.

In addition, each person writes (with adequate detail) the list of responsibilities that are part of his / her role. The following is an example of a role and responsibilities statement.

Role and Responsibilities

Role: Manage team's activities toward "our" goal

Responsibilities:

- Oversee contract negotiation
- Develop strategy for uninterrupted, safe and economical service
- Provide our team's input for future plans
- Coordinate all team activity toward common, efficient goal
- Sign off on specs
- Advertise our services
- Investigate alternatives for improved service
- Support team in daily operations
- Develop strategy for continuous improvement
- Develop personnel – career opportunities, educational assistance
- Be available for team concerns
- Create or help create open communication with other teams
- Represent our team in the department and company
- Develop the team

Often there are responsibilities that have not been clearly assigned. Team members should list those as "Gray Areas." This will help the whole team confront overlaps as well as gaps in assigned responsibilities.

One by one, individuals read their list to the others. Team members can ask for more details, or for clarification, or challenge what has been listed. There may be certain items that cannot be immediately agreed upon. These items should be recorded as a "Follow–Up" list on a flip chart.

When an organization goes through restructuring, it is important for the team members to identify which of their responsibilities have now gone away. This should lead to the team asking, "Is there still a need for this to be done?" If the answer is "yes," then a second question is appropriate, "Is our team still responsible or does this responsibility now belong to some other team?" Depending on the answer to this question, action needs to be taken to assure the responsibility is reassigned, preventing it from "falling through the cracks."

When every team member, including the Team Leader / Manager, has completed this process, the finalized list of each person's role and responsibilities should be compiled and distributed to all (and to other teams or individuals as appropriate).

Depending on the number of team members, this exercise can range from a couple of hours to a full day.

II. Developing Your Team Action Plan

The next agenda item is to develop the Team Action Plan. For each of the Key Improvement Areas, the team members will generate specific action items that will lead to improvement, select the best ones, list them in a sequential order, clearly assign responsibilities, and establish deadlines.

In developing their Action Plan, the team members should strive for "SMART" action items:

S = **Specific** - the action items must clearly describe the desired behaviors / actions

M = **Measurable** - the action items must be measurable (Did we do this? How well? Etc.)

A = **Achievable** - the actions must be realistic and achievable given the resources available

R = **Relevant** - the actions must be important to improving the team's KIAs

T = **Time-based** - deadlines must be established. Without them, little or nothing gets done

It is easy for teams to get carried away in developing their Action Plan. The purpose is not to develop the longest, most comprehensive, most complicated Action Plan in history. On the contrary, the best Action Plan is one that requires the least amount of time and effort to create significant improvements in the team's effectiveness.

The team leader can play an important role by cautioning the team to use the "KISS" approach (Keep It Short and Simple), and ***reminding them that he / she expects the team to implement any actions that are developed***. Holding team members accountable for their action items is likely to result in a much better and more realistic Action Plan.

A good way to streamline the action planning process is to break the team into several small groups and assign one KIA to each group. The group will be responsible for taking the first cut at generating, selecting and listing action items to improve on their KIA. The group will then present their ideas to the entire team, and all team members will collaborate to finalize action steps, set deadlines and clarify responsibilities.

In setting deadlines, it is important to keep the time-frame relatively short - preferably 30 to 90 days. In reality, some action items cannot be fully implemented in three months. Nevertheless, we believe that setting short-term deadlines, progress reviews, status checks, etc., is likely to keep the momentum flowing.

Also, in establishing who is responsible for implementing the action items, we have a few words of caution:

- Avoid assigning responsibility for specific action items to "All." Our experience tells us that "All" means no one. Even if the efforts of several or all team members will be required in order to implement the action item, assigning the responsibility to one person - and then holding that person accountable for results – will increase the likelihood of success.

- Make sure that the assignment of responsibilities is distributed among all team members. Some team members will likely end up with more responsibilities than others, but the team should strive to assign some actions to all team members and not overload any one person.

- The team leader should not allow the group to assign a disproportionate share of the action items to him or her. Instead, the leader should strive to "put the monkey on their backs" unless the particular action requires the leader's involvement.

Selecting a "Champion" for each KIA

It is important to select a "Champion" for each KIA. The Champion should be a person who is passionate about the KIA, is knowledgeable and experienced on the subject, and is willing to devote the necessary time and effort to ensure success. The Champion's responsibilities are to:

1. Lead the effort
2. Keep people motivated
3. Make sure progress is reviewed on a regular basis
4. Provide feedback on progress
5. Recognize contributions of team members
6. Take corrective action if team gets behind schedule
7. Make sure success is celebrated

It is best to have different people serve as Champions for each KIA addressed in the Action Plan.

After the Action Plan has been finalized, a copy should be distributed to all team members and to the manager(s) of the team leader. Openly communicating what the team intends to do increases commitment to success.

A typical Action Planning Form follows.

Team: ______________________________

KIA: ______________________________

Champion: ______________________________

ACTION PLAN

Action Steps: What Do You Intend to Do?	By When?	By Whom?
1. ______________________________	________	________
2. ______________________________	________	________
3. ______________________________	________	________
4 ______________________________	________	________
5. ______________________________	________	________
6. ______________________________	________	________
7. ______________________________	________	________

III. Developing the Team Charter

Another effective tool for building the commitment of team members during a team building retreat is to develop a "Team Charter." This is a document that spells out the guidelines or behaviors expected by team members. It gives the team a structure to follow based on a set of norms or standards that support their continuing effectiveness. The list of behaviors and guidelines should be developed and accepted by all the team members.

The team, working in small groups, should list what they expect of each other to ensure the success of the team, focusing both on the task ahead and on the process of interaction. After considering each group's list, the team agrees to a single list of expectations.

There should be a brief reminder by the facilitator that all team members need to commit to these guidelines and that it is the responsibility of the team to hold each other accountable for observing them. When team members do not follow these norms, it is the responsibility of one of the team members to call for a "time out" and open a discussion of the issue(s) among the team members.

The following are excellent examples of team charters.

TEAM CHARTER – EXAMPLE 1

The following are the rules we have agreed will guide our team interaction:

- We will continuously clarify our team objectives and work to achieve them.
- Everyone will have a clearly defined role to achieve the team's objectives.
- Our team will meet quarterly.
- We will distribute an agenda for meetings ahead of time so people can come prepared.
- All team members who can be available will be expected to attend the quarterly meeting with a minimum of 7 team members required for problem solving / decision making meetings.
- There must be a representative from Operations, Maintenance, and Administration.
- Decisions made by team participants at a team meeting will be binding for all.
- We will have a code of conduct in the areas of:
  - Responsibility
  - Punctuality
  - Conflict resolution
  - Discipline

- We will record meeting decisions, deadlines, and responsibilities.
- Periodically we will conduct an assessment of team performance in the areas of:
  - Mission, KRAs, KIAs, etc.
  - How the group is functioning as a team
  - Productivity
  - Quality and customer satisfaction

TEAMWORK

THE WAY A TEAM PLAYS DETERMINES ITS SUCCESS. YOU MAY HAVE THE GREATEST BUNCH OF INDIVIDUAL STARS IN THE WORLD, BUT IF THEY DON'T PLAY WELL TOGETHER, THE TEAM WON'T BE WORTH A DIME.

BABE RUTH,
BASEBALL LEGEND

TEAM CHARTER - EXAMPLE 2

Behaviors Expected of Team Members

- Be familiar with team goals and objectives
- Understand your role and responsibilities
- Continuously improve skills
- Establish performance standards
- Strive for technical excellence
- Seek and provide mentoring when appropriate
- Actively cooperate with other teams
- Communicate openly (up, down and sideways)
- Listen to others
- Honor commitments (timelines, quality, etc.)
- Provide and seek feedback to / from other team members
- Support each other's ideas and efforts
- Be willing to change
- Strive for consensus
- Show initiative / be self-motivated

Behaviors Expected of Team Leader

- Be a good listener
- Provide direction and focus on goals and objectives
- Encourage teamwork
- Delegate effectively (empowerment)
- Provide and encourage timely feedback
- Be flexible / willing to change
- Set realistic deadlines
- Motivate and be supportive
- Ensure fairness
- Make decisions in a timely manner
- Provide effective staff training and development
- Defend team's actions
- When giving feedback, focus on the positive first
- Allow reasonable risk-taking
- Ensure effective communication within and outside of team (up, down, sideways)
- Provide timely rewards and recognition
- Build a trusting environment
- Strive for effective resolution of conflicts
- Ensure effective planning and prioritizing of work
- Ensure cooperation with other teams
- Be a positive role model

Meeting Rules

- Have a meeting only if needed
- Prepare agenda
- Provide appropriate advance notice and information
- Start and end on time
- Be punctual and prepared
- Designate a Facilitator, Recorder and Timekeeper
- Keep meeting short
- Keep meeting on track
- Solicit input from all
- Be clear and concise
- Allow only one conversation at a time
- Don't interrupt others
- Follow agenda
- Strive for consensus (when appropriate)
- Plan next meeting
- Clarify accountability for assigned tasks
- Distribute meeting report promptly

IV. Implementing the Team Action Plan

At the end of the team building session, a half hour or so should be devoted to discussing how to ensure the successful implementation of the Team Action Plan. A list of "Keys to Successful Implementation" should be developed by the team. A sample list is provided below.

Keys to Successful Implementation of Our Action Plan

- Clarify role of the "Champions" and team members who have been assigned action items
- Identify and commit resources
- Define milestones and check to assess timely progress
- Have brief status / progress reports in weekly / monthly team meetings
- Hold people accountable for their assigned action items
- Celebrate success
- Update Action Plan every three to six months

> **THE WORLD'S BEST PLAN IS WORTHLESS WITHOUT EXECUTION.**
>
> **JACK WELCH, FORMER CEO GENERAL ELECTRIC**

V. Planning Your Team Building Progress Review

A sad fact about Team Building workshops is that many well-designed and effective Action Plans do not get implemented. As soon as team members get back to their jobs, it is very easy for them to get caught up in their old habits and activity traps, and within a few weeks the Action Plan has been forgotten. It is crucial for the team to recognize that plans without execution have no value.

Developing the "Keys to Successful Implementation" (discussed in the previous section) is helpful. But to increase the likelihood that the Action Plan will be implemented, we recommend scheduling a half-day Team Building Progress Review before concluding the Team Building Workshop. The Progress Review should normally take place one to three months later. As mentioned earlier, the leader should stress that to improve as a team, the plan must be implemented, and that team members – including the team leader – will be held accountable for fulfilling their responsibilities.

As the Progress Review date approaches, the team leader should remind team members to implement their assigned actions and come to the session prepared to review progress. The agenda for the Progress Review should also be planned and communicated to the team members. A sample agenda is listed below.

Team Building Progress Review

I. Review Team Mission

II. Review Team Key Results Areas (KRAs)

III. Review Team Key Improvement Areas (KIAs)

IV. Review Progress on Team Action Plan

  A. KIA 1

  B. KIA 2

  C. KIA 3, etc.

V. Discussion of New Issues / Problems / Concerns

VI. Update Team Action Plan

VII. Recognize Individual Contributions and Celebrate Team Successes

A docked Russian Soyuz Spacecraft (right) backdropped by the thin line of Earth's atmosphere and the blackness of space is featured in this image, which was taken by the STS-133 crew. The image also features a portion of the International Space Station's Quest airlock and solar array panels.(March 2011)

Photo courtesy of NASA, Johnson Space Center

CHAPTER 4

REVIEWING AND RENEWING YOUR TEAM BUILDING EFFORTS

REVIEWING YOUR TEAM'S PROGRESS

The purpose of the Team Building Progress Review is to ensure that the team is increasing its effectiveness and implementing the Team Action Plan. As outlined above, the session should begin with a brief review of the Team's Mission, KRAs and KIAs. Normally these will not be altered at this stage because only one to three months have passed since they were developed. However, if there has been a significant change in the responsibilities of the team, the Mission, KRAs and KIAs should be revised accordingly.

The Team Action Plan should then be reviewed in detail. We suggest that copies of the Action Plan be distributed to team members. Each KIA and its respective Action Steps should be reviewed, including:

- Planned Action Steps
- Actual Progress on Each Step
- Recognition for the Contributions of Team Members and Others Involved
- Problems Encountered
- Discussion of What Remains to be Done

Any incomplete or additional action steps should be recorded for inclusion in the revised Action Plan.

The team should then discuss any new issues, problems or concerns that have emerged since the Team Building Workshop and decide if the Team Action Plan should be expanded to include additional Key Improvement Areas. If so, the team should brainstorm action steps, select and prioritize them, and assign deadlines and responsibilities in the same manner utilized with the original KIAs in the previous session.

Before adjourning, the revised Action Plan should be reviewed and the leader and team members should voice their support for the plan and their continuing commitment to its successful implementation. Another progress review should be scheduled within six months.

CONTINUING THE TEAM BUILDING PROCESS

With a high level of involvement and commitment by the team leader and members, the team should have made a great deal of progress toward becoming a "High Performance Team." It is important to keep the process alive by dedicating some time on an ongoing basis to team building activities. We recommend that the team schedule a team building retreat for at least one day on an annual basis. In those sessions, the team's effectiveness should be re-assessed (using a Team Effectiveness Survey). Also, the Team's Mission, KRAs and KIAs should be reviewed and updated. Finally, the Team Action Plan should be revised to re-energize the team's enthusiasm and commitment. By taking these steps, team excellence and continuous improvement will become a way of life for your "High Performing Team."

NOT THE END!

Inside the U.S. lab Destiny, 12 astronauts and cosmonauts take a break from a very busy week aboard the International Space Station for a joint STS-133/Expedition 26 group portrait on March 3, 2011.

Photo courtesy of NASA

DO IT NOW!

YOU BECOME SUCCESSFUL THE MOMENT YOU START MOVING TOWARD A WORTHWHILE GOAL.

Overall view of the space station flight control room in Houston's JSC Mission Control Center (August 11, 2010).

Photo courtesy of NASA, Johnson Space Center

**TEAMWORK IS THE ABILITY
TO WORK TOGETHER
TOWARD A COMMON VISION.**

**THE ABILITY TO DIRECT INDIVIDUAL
ACCOMPLISHMENTS TOWARD
ORGANIZATIONAL OBJECTIVES.**

**IT IS THE FUEL THAT ALLOWS
COMMON PEOPLE TO ATTAIN
UNCOMMON RESULTS.**

**ANDREW CARNEGIE,
INDUSTRIALIST, BUSINESSMAN,
ENTREPRENEUR AND
MAJOR PHILANTHROPIST**

RECOMMENDED READINGS

The Wisdom of Teams

The Characteristics of a High Performance Team

Conquering the Five Dysfunctions of a Team

The Wisdom of Teams

Jon R. Katzenbach
Douglas K. Smith

Why Teams?

Teams have existed for hundreds of years, are the subject of countless books, and have been celebrated throughout many countries and cultures. Most people believe they know how teams work as well as the benefits teams offer. Many have had first-hand team experiences themselves, some of which were rewarding and others a waste of time. Yet, as we explored the use of teams, it became increasingly clear that the potential impact of single teams, as well as the collective impact of many teams, on the performance of large organizations is woefully underexploited—despite the rapidly growing recognition of the need for what teams have to offer. Understanding this paradox and the discipline required to deal with it are central to the basic lessons we learned about team performance.

Reprinted by permission of Harvard Business School Press. From The Wisdom of Teams *by Jon R. Katzenbach and Douglas K. Smith. Boston, MA 1993, pp. 11-26.*

LESSONS WE LEARNED

Initially, we thought that executives and other decision makers could make teams work if only they understood the compelling argument for why teams make a difference to performance. We learned the challenge is more difficult than that. Most people, particularly business executives, already recognize the value in teams. Long-standing habits, demanding time schedules, and unwarranted assumptions, however, seem to prevent them from taking full advantage of team opportunities.

We also thought that people understood most of what differentiated a team from a nonteam, and therefore, only needed a clearer definition of terms to take full advantage of teams. We discovered instead that most people simply do not apply what they already know about teams in any disciplined way and thereby miss the performance potential within existing teams, much less seek out new potential team opportunities.

There is much more to the wisdom of teams than we ever expected, which we highlight in the following summary of key lessons we have learned about teams and team performance.

1. Significant performance challenges energize teams regardless of where they are in an organization. No team arises without a performance challenge that is meaningful to those involved. Good personal chemistry or the desire to "become a team," for example, can foster teamwork values, but teamwork is not the same thing as a team. Rather, a common set of demanding performance goals that a group considers important to achieve will lead, most of the time, to both performance and a team. Performance, however, is the primary objective *while a team remains the means, not the end.*

Performance is the crux of the matter for teams. Its importance applies to many different groupings, including teams who recommend things, teams who make or do things, and teams who run or manage things. Each of these three types of teams do face unique challenges. Teams that make or do things often need to develop new skills for managing themselves as compared to teams elsewhere in organizations. Teams that recommend things often find their biggest challenge comes when they make the handoff to those who must implement their findings. Finally, groups who run or manage things must address hierarchical obstacles and turf issues more than groups who recommend, make, or do things. But notwithstanding such special issues, any team—if it focuses on performance regardless of where it is in an organization or what it does—will deliver results well beyond what individuals acting alone in nonteam working situations could achieve.

---

2. Organizational leaders can foster team performance best by building a strong performance ethic rather than by establishing a team-promoting environment alone. A performance focus is also critical to what we learned about how leaders create organizational environments that are friendly to teams. In fact, too many executives fall into the trap of appearing to promote teams for the sake of teams. They talk about entire organizations becoming a "team" and thereby equate teams with teamwork. Or they reorganize their companies around self-managing teams, and risk putting the number of officially designated teams as an objective ahead of performance. They sometimes loosely refer to their own small group at the top as a team when most people in the organization recognize that they are anything but a team.

Real teams are much more likely to flourish if leaders aim their sights on performance results that balance the needs of customers, employees, and shareholders. Clarity of purpose and goals have tremendous power in our ever more change-driven world. Most people, at all organizational levels, understand that job security depends on customer satisfaction and financial performance, and are willing to be measured and rewarded accordingly. What is perhaps less well appreciated, but equally true, is how the opportunity to meet clearly stated customer and financial needs enriches jobs and leads to personal growth.

Most of us really do want to make a difference. Naturally, organization policies, designs, and processes that promote teams can accelerate team-based performance in companies already blessed with strong performance cultures. But in those organizations with weak performance ethics or cultures, leaders will provide a sounder foundation for teams by addressing and demanding performance than by embracing the latest organization design fad, including teams themselves.

3. Biases toward individualism exist but need not get in the way of team performance. Most of us grew up with a strong sense of individual responsibility. Parents, teachers, coaches, and role models of all kinds shape our values based on individual accomplishment. Rugged individualism is credited with the formation of our country and our political society. These same values carry through in our corporate families, where all advancement and reward systems are based on individual evaluations. Even when teams are part of the picture, it is seldom at the expense of individual achievement. We are taught to play fair, but "Always look out for number one!" And, most of us have taken this to heart far more deeply than sentiments such as "We're all in this together" or "If one fails, we all fail."

Self-preservation and individual accountability, however, can work two ways. Left unattended, they can preclude or destroy potential teams. But recognized and addressed for what they are, especially if done with reference to how to meet a performance challenge, individual concerns and differences become a source of collective strength. Teams are not antithetical to individual performance. Real teams always find ways for each individual to contribute and thereby gain distinction. Indeed, when harnessed to a common team purpose and goals, our need to distinguish ourselves as individuals becomes a powerful engine for team performance. Nothing we learned in looking at dozens of teams supports an argument for the wholesale abandonment of the individual in favor of teams.

4. Discipline—both within the team and across the organization—creates the conditions for team performance. Any group seeking team performance for itself, like any leader seeking to build strong performance standards across his organization, must focus sharply on performance. For organizational leaders, this entails making clear and consistent demands that reflect the needs of customers, shareholders, and employees, and then holding themselves and the organization relentlessly accountable. Out of such demands come the most fruitful conditions for teams. An analogous lesson also applies to teams. Indeed, we think of the team definition not as a series of elements characterizing teams but as a discipline, much like a diet, that, if followed rigorously, will produce the conditions for team performance. Groups become teams through *disciplined action*. They *shape* a common purpose, *agree* on performance goals, *define* a common working approach, *develop* high levels of complementary skills, and *hold* themselves mutually accountable for results. And, as with any effective discipline, they never stop doing any of these things.

The Need for Teams

We believe that teams—real teams, not just groups that management calls "teams"—should be the basic unit of performance for most organizations, regardless of size. In any situation requiring the real-time combination of multiple skills, experiences, and judgments, a team inevitably gets better results than a collection of individuals operating within confined job roles and responsibilities. Teams are more flexible than larger organizational groupings because they can be more quickly assembled, deployed, refocused, and disbanded, usually in ways that enhance rather than disrupt more permanent structures and processes. Teams are more productive than groups that have no clear performance objectives because their members are committed to deliver tangible performance results. Teams and performance are an unbeatable combination.

Teams and performance are an unbeatable combination.

Resistance to Teams

We believe the argument for greater focus on teams is compelling, and most people we have interviewed agree. Yet when it comes to using the team approach for themselves or those they manage, most of these same people are reluctant to rely on teams. Notwithstanding the evidence of team performance all around us, the importance of teams in managing behavioral change and high performance, and the rewards of team experiences in everyday lives, many people undervalue, forget, or openly question the team option when confronting their own performance challenges. We cannot fully explain this resistance; there probably are as many reasons and emotions as there are people. Moreover, we do not suggest that such resistance is either "bad" or "good." We do, however, think that it is powerful because it is grounded in deeply held values of individualism that neither can nor should be entirely dismissed.

Three primary sources for people's reluctance about teams stand out: a lack of conviction that a team or teams can work better than other alternatives; personal styles, capabilities, and preferences that make teams risky or uncomfortable; and weak organizational performance ethics that discourage the conditions in which teams flourish.

1. Lack of conviction. Some people do not believe that teams, except in unusual or unpredictable circumstances, really do perform better than individuals. Some think that teams cause more trouble than they are worth because the members waste time in unproductive meetings and discussions, and actually generate more complaints than constructive results. Others think that teams are probably useful from a human relations point of view, but are a hindrance when it comes to work, productivity, and decisive action. Still others believe that concepts of teamwork and empowerment applied broadly to an organization supersede the need to worry or be disciplined about the performance of specific small groups of people.

On the one hand, most people share a lot of constructive common sense about teams but fail to rigorously apply it. People know, for example, that teams rarely work without common goals; yet far too many teams casually accept goals that are neither demanding, precise, realistic, nor actually held *in common*. On the other hand, the very popularity of the word "team" courts imprecision. People rarely use "team" with much concern for its specific meaning to them in the context they face. As a consequence, most people remain unclear over what makes a real team. A team is not just any group working together. Committees, councils, and task forces are not necessarily teams. Groups do not become teams simply because someone labels them as teams. The complete workforce of any large and complex organization is never a team. Entire organizations can believe in and practice teamwork, but teamwork and teams differ.

Most executives outspokenly advocate teamwork. And they should. Teamwork represents a set of values that encourages behaviors such as listening and constructively responding to points of view expressed by others, giving others the benefit of the doubt, providing support to those who need it, and recognizing the interests and achievements of others. When practiced, such values help all of us communicate and work more effectively with one another and, therefore, are good and valuable behaviors. Obviously, teamwork values help teams perform. They also promote our performance as individuals and the performance of the entire organization. In other words, teamwork values—by themselves—are not exclusive to teams, nor are they enough to ensure team performance.

Teams are discrete units of performance, not a positive set of values. And they are a unit of performance that differs from the individual or the entire organization. A team is a small group of people (typically fewer than twenty) with complementary skills committed to a common purpose and set of specific performance goals. Its members are committed to working with each other to achieve the team's purpose and hold each other fully and jointly accountable for the team's results. Teamwork encourages and helps teams succeed; but teamwork alone never makes a team. Consequently, when senior executives call for the entire organization to be a "team," they really are promoting teamwork values. However well intended, such ambiguities can cause unproductive confusion. Moreover, those who describe teams as vehicles primarily to make people feel good or get along better not only confuse teamwork with teams, but also miss the most fundamental characteristic that distinguishes real teams from nonteams—a relentless focus on performance.

Teams thrive on performance challenges; they flounder without them. Teams cannot exist for long without a performance-driven purpose to both nourish and justify the team's continuing existence. Groups established for the sake of becoming a team, job enhancement, communication, organizational effectiveness, or even excellence rarely become real teams, as demonstrated by the bad feelings left in many companies after experimenting with quality circles. While quality represents an admirable aspiration, quality circles often fail to connect specific, achievable performance objectives with the collaborative effort of those in the circle.

Ignoring performance, we suspect, also explains much of the evidence about apparent team failures. Peter Drucker, for example, has cited the difficulties GM, P&G, and Xerox, among others, have had in overshooting the mark with "team-building" efforts. Without question, teams and team efforts sometimes fail. But more often than not, such failures lie in not adhering to the discipline of what makes teams successful. In other words, unclear thinking and practice explain more about such disappointments than whether teams are appropriate units of performance to get something done. Regardless of their cause, however, such unrewarding personal experiences in groups labeled as teams weaken people's conviction about teams even further. Many of us who have observed, participated in, or watched the best intentions at team-building exercises get quickly forgotten or scorned have grown cynical, cautious, or even hostile to teams.

2. Personal discomfort and risk. Many people fear or do not like to work in teams. Some are true loners who contribute best when left to work quietly on their own. Some research scientists, university professors, and specialized consultants fit this pattern. Most people's discomfort with teams, however, is because they find the team approach too time-consuming, too uncertain, or too risky.

"My job is tough enough," goes one recurring comment, "without having to worry about meeting and getting along with a bunch of people I don't even know that well, or I do know and I'm not sure I like all that much. I just don't have that kind of time to invest." In this view, teams represent a risky extra burden that can slow down individual accomplishment and advancement. Some people are uncomfortable about speaking up, participating, or being otherwise conspicuous in group settings. Some are afraid of making commitments that they might not be able to keep. And many people just do not like the idea of having to depend on others, having to listen or agree to contrary points of view, or having to suffer the consequences of other people's mistakes. These concerns particularly afflict managers who find it difficult to be part of a team when they are not the leader.

Few people deny the benefit of teamwork values or the potentially useful performance impact of teams. But, at their core, most people have values that favor individual responsibility and performance over any form of group, whether it be a team or otherwise. Our parents, teachers, ministers, and other elders emphasize individual responsibility as paramount from our earliest days onward. We grow up under a regimen that measures (academic grades), rewards (allowances), and punishes (trips to the principal's office) individual—not collective—performance. Whenever we want to "get something done," our first thought is that of holding an individual responsible.

It is hardly surprising, then, to discover strong anxieties among individuals faced with joining a team. It is not that teams and teamwork are absent from our culture. From *The Three Musketeers* through *The Dirty Dozen* and *Star Trek*, we have read about, listened to, and watched stories of famous teams accomplishing the improbable. Most sports we follow are team sports. And our parents and other teachers have also instructed us in, and expected us to practice, teamwork values. But for most of us, these admirable notions, however potentially rewarding, forever remain secondary to our responsibilities as individuals. Individual responsibility and self-preservation remain the rule; shared responsibility based on trusting others is the exception. A reluctance to take a risk and submit one's fate to the performance of a team, therefore, is almost inbred.

3. Weak organizational performance ethics. The reluctance to commit one's own fate to a team pervades most organizations with weak performance ethics. Such companies lack compelling purposes that appeal rationally and emotionally to their people. Their leaders fail to make clear and meaningful performance demands to which they hold the organization and, most important, themselves accountable. To the organization at large, such behavior manifests more concern about internal politics or external public relations than a commitment to a clear set of goals that balances the expectations of customers, shareholders, and employees. At the worst, such environments undermine the mutual trust and openness upon which teams depend. There is a built-in expectation that any decision of consequence must be made at the top or, at a minimum, be approved by enough other layers that the implementor of that decision is well-covered. Politics displace performance as the daily focus. And, inevitably, those politics play on individual insecurities that, in turn, further erode the conviction and courage to invest in a team approach. Bad team experiences become self-fulfilling prophecies.

Modifying the strong natural emphasis on individual accountability will, of course, be necessary as teams become more important. ***Yet replacing individually focused management structures and approaches with team-oriented designs will matter little, or even do damage, unless the organization has a robust performance ethic.*** If it does, then shifting the organization's emphasis away from individual toward team can enrich both the number and performance of teams—particularly if management also is disciplined about how it deals with team situations. But all the team-promoting policies in the world will fall short if the teams are not convinced that performance truly matters. Some teams, of course, will always emerge—beyond all reasonable expectation. But they will remain the exception. Because of the all-important link between teams and performance, companies with weak performance ethics will always breed resistance to teams themselves.

TEAMS THRIVE ON PERFORMANCE CHALLENGES; THEY FLOUNDER WITHOUT THEM.

Conclusion

Teams are *not* the solution to everyone's current and future organizational needs. They will not solve every problem, enhance every group's results, nor help top management address every performance challenge. Moreover, when misapplied, they can be both wasteful and disruptive. Nonetheless, teams usually do outperform other groups and individuals. They represent one of the best ways to support the broad-based changes necessary for the high-performing organization. And executives who really believe that behaviorally-based characteristics like quality, innovation, cost effectiveness, and customer service will help build sustainable competitive advantage will give top priority to the development of team performance.

To succeed, however, they and others must also pay a lot of attention to why most people approach teams cautiously. In large part, this resistance springs from undeniable experiences and convictions about individual responsibility and the risks involved in trusting other people. Teams, for example, do demand a merging of individual accountability with mutual accountability. Teams also do require lots of time together; indeed, it is folly to assume that teams can perform without investing time to shape and agree upon a common purpose, set of goals, and working approach. Moreover, few groups become real teams without taking risks to overcome constraints imposed by individual, functional, and hierarchical boundaries. And team members do depend on one another in pursuit of common performance.

No wonder, then, that many of us only reluctantly entrust critical issues to team resolution. We all fool ourselves if we think well-meaning aspirations to "work better as a team" will be enough to dispel the resistance to teams.

Building the performance of teams throughout an organization that needs to perform better, we argue, is mandatory. But doing so also poses a far more serious challenge than any of us would like to admit.

The good news is that there is a discipline to teams that, if rigorously followed, can transform reluctance into team performance. Moreover, while some of the elements of this discipline are counter-intuitive and must be learned—for example, that "becoming a team" is not the primary goal—most of it builds on common sense ideas like the importance of goal setting and mutual accountability. Furthermore, this discipline applies equally well to teams that run things, teams that recommend things, and teams that make or do things. What works at the front lines also works in the executive suite.

The bad news is that, like all disciplines, the price of success is strict adherence and practice. Very few people lose weight, quit smoking, or learn the piano or golf without constant practice and discipline. Very few small groups of people become teams without discipline as well. Extracting team performance is challenging. Long-standing habits of individualism, rampant confusion about teams and teamwork, and seemingly adverse team experiences all undercut the possibilities teams offer at the very moment that team performance has become so critical. Groups do not become teams just because we tell them to; launching hundreds of teams will not necessarily produce real teams in the right places; and building teams at the top remains among the most difficult of tests. Yet the fact remains that potential teams throughout most organizations usually can perform much better than they do. We believe this untapped potential literally begs for renewed attention, especially from the top. We also believe the key to such performance is in recognizing the wisdom of teams, having the courage to try, and then applying the discipline to learn from the experience.

The Characteristics of a High Performance Team

Pat MacMillan

For most of us, positive team experiences are rare. If you have been part of an extraordinary team in the past, you will probably long for that experience again. People often drift into and then out of extraordinary team situations, wondering what made that group "click" and how to replicate it. A key first step to more predictable and enhanced team performance is understanding the common characteristics of teams that consistently achieve exceptional results.

As we have studied and researched teams and teamwork over the years, we have found consistently similar qualities and characteristics in teams that achieve exceptional results. This list of characteristics has proven to be of immeasurable value as we have worked with clients to establish new teams or to intervene when team effort was less than effective. It's a short list; in fact, it contains only six characteristics. But each characteristic plays a specific and vital role in making the team effective, and therefore it is worth a closer look. If one of these six characteristics is missing or inadequate, the team is, at best, limping. If two or three are lacking, this group is probably not a team at all.

---

1. Common Purpose

The single most important ingredient in team success is a clear, common, compelling task. The power of a team flows out of each team member's alignment to its purpose. The task of any team is to accomplish an objective and to do so at exceptional levels of performance. Teams are not ends in themselves but rather means to an end. Therefore, high performance teams will be purpose directed, ultimately judged by their results.

2. Crystal Clear Roles

High performance teams are characterized by crystal clear roles. Every team member is clear about his or her particular role, as well as those of the other team members. Roles are about how we design, divide, and deploy the work of the team. While the concept is compellingly logical, many teams find it very challenging to implement in practice. There is often a tendency to take role definition to extremes or not take it far enough. However, when they get it right, team members discover that making their combination more effective and leveraging their collective efforts is an important key to synergistic results.

If you have been part of an extraordinary team in the past, you will probably long for that experience again.

3. Accepted Leadership

High performance teams need clear, competent leadership. When such leadership is lacking, groups lose their way. Whereas a common, compelling task might be the biggest contributor to team effectiveness, inadequate team leadership may be the single biggest reason for team ineffectiveness. Teams are, in the very truest sense, volunteers. Volunteers are not managed, but they demand *accepted* leadership capable of calling out the levels of initiative and creativity that motivate exceptional levels of both individual and collective performance.

4. Effective Processes

Teams and processes go together. Many professions take processes for granted. It would never occur to a surgical team, construction crew, string quartet, film crew, or the team on the flight deck of Flight 232 to approach their tasks without clearly defined processes. The playbook of a football team or the score sheet of a string quartet clearly outlines their processes. Business teams have processes as well. Instead of a run off tackle, or executing the scene in Act II, such processes might include making decisions, managing a meeting, processing insurance claims, or any other activities we undertake in pursuit of our mission. Hopefully, in each of these group processes each team member has a clear, specific role based on their function, skills, and expertise. In many business settings, however, such processes are often ill-defined or missing entirely. High performance teams identify, map, and then master their key team processes. They constantly evaluate the effectiveness of key processes, asking: How are we doing? What are we learning? How can we do it better?

5. Solid Relationships

One of the biggest misperceptions I find in the world of teams and teamwork is the belief that to work and communicate effectively, team members must be close comrades. Not true. In fact, the diversity of skill, experience, and knowledge needed to effectively and creatively divide the task almost precludes high levels of friendship, which is most often based in common interests.

Speaking of diversity, we find that the more different a team is, the smarter it can be. A team whose members look at the world through different lenses of function, gender, ethnicity, personality, experience, and perspective has a decided advantage over a more homogenous group. The diverse group will be able to surround problems, decisions, and other team issues with a brighter collective IQ. They will see more solutions and more creative solutions if they can channel their differences into synergy rather than strife.

Because diversity provides plenty of opportunity for discord, conflict, and communication breakdowns, especially among teams that must accomplish their tasks in complex, high velocity, dynamic environments, their differences must be offset by trust, acceptance, respect, courtesy, and a liberal dose of understanding.

6. Excellent Communication

Communication is the very means of cooperation. One of the primary motives for companies to implement teams is that team-based organizations are more responsive and move faster. A team, or the organization in which it resides, cannot move faster than it communicates. Fast, clear, accurate communication is a hallmark of high levels of team performance.

Effective teams have mastered the art of straight talk; there is little wasted motion from misunderstanding and confusion. Ideas move like quicksilver. The team understands that effective communication is key to thinking collectively and finding synergy in team solutions. As a result they approach communication with a determined intentionality. They talk about it a lot and put a lot of effort into keeping it good and getting better.

When it comes to teams, these six characteristics are the lightning in the bottle. If a team gets these few things right, they will realize exceptional results. By effectively applying the principles and practices, teams will avoid many of the pitfalls and problems that derail many team initiatives.

Message to Team Leaders

If these few characteristics are critical to team success, you, the team leader, are critical to these characteristics.

- The team leader helps the team clarify the task and align behind it.
- The team leader has the power to call the time out needed to allow the team members to clarify roles and the authority to resolve conflict when they can't agree about who does what.
- The team leader must earn the acceptance of team members. The only boss of a team is the task; if you want your team members to serve the task, you must learn how to serve them. Volunteers, and that's what every team member is, will only respond to leaders they accept.
- High performance teams have high performance processes. Again, it is generally the team leader who can create the time and space for the team to identify and design its processes as well as evaluate its effectiveness on a regular basis.
- Team leaders model the qualities of effective team relationships and create opportunities for the team to develop the needed levels of trust, respect, and acceptance.
- Team leaders must create an environment that fosters open, clear, accurate communication—communication that clears the way for exceptional levels of creativity and that allows the team to efficiently implement its processes and move quickly against problems and decisions.

Conquering the Five Dysfunctions of a Team

By Patrick Lencioni

Like it or not, all teams are potentially dysfunctional. This is inevitable because they are made up of fallible, imperfect human beings. From the basketball court to the executive suite, politics and confusion are more the rule than the exception. However, facing dysfunction and focusing on teamwork is particularly critical at the top of an organization because the executive team sets the tone for how all employees work with one another.

A former client, the founder of a billion dollar company, best expressed the power of teamwork when he once told me, "If you could get all the people in the organization rowing in the same direction, you could dominate any industry, in any market, against any competition, at any time."

Whenever I repeat this adage to a group of leaders, they immediately nod their heads, but in a desperate sort of way. They seem to grasp the truth of it while simultaneously surrendering to the impossibility of actually making it happen.

Patrick Lencioni is the founder and president of The Table Group, a firm dedicated to providing organizations with ideas, products, and services that improve teamwork, clarity, and employee engagement. Lencioni is the author of nine best-selling books with nearly 3 million copies sold. After nine years in print, his book The Five Dysfunctions of a Team *continues to be a fixture on national best-seller lists.*

Fortunately, there is hope. Counter to conventional wisdom, the causes of dysfunction are both identifiable and curable. However, they don't die easily. Making a team functional and cohesive requires levels of courage and discipline that many groups cannot seem to muster.

ADDRESSING THE DYSFUNCTIONS

To begin improving your team and to better understand the level of dysfunction you are facing, ask yourself these simple questions:

- Do team members openly and readily disclose their opinions?
- Are team meetings compelling and productive?
- Does the team come to decisions quickly and avoid getting bogged down by consensus?
- Do team members confront one another about their short-comings?
- Do team members sacrifice their own interests for the good of the team?

Although no team is perfect and even the best teams sometimes struggle with one or more of these issues, the finest organizations constantly work to ensure that their answers are "yes." If you answered "no" to many of these questions, your team may need some work.

The first step toward reducing politics and confusion within your team is to understand that there are five dysfunctions to contend with, and address each that applies, one by one.

The Dysfunctions

Dysfunction #1: Absence of Trust

This occurs when team members are reluctant to be vulnerable with one another and are unwilling to admit their mistakes, weaknesses or needs for help. Without a certain comfort level among team members, a foundation of trust is impossible.

Dysfunction #2: Fear of Conflict

Teams that are lacking on trust are incapable of engaging in unfiltered, passionate debate about key issues, causing situations where team conflict can easily turn into veiled discussions and back channel comments. In a work setting where team members do not openly air their opinions, inferior decisions are the result.

Dysfunction #3: Lack of Commitment

Without conflict, it is difficult for team members to commit to decisions, creating an environment where ambiguity prevails. Lack of direction and commitment can make employees, particularly star employees, disgruntled.

Dysfunction #4: Avoidance of Accountability

When teams don't commit to a clear plan of action, even the most focused and driven individuals hesitate to call their peers on actions and behaviors that may seem counterproductive to the overall good of the team.

Dysfunction #5: Inattention to Results

Team members naturally tend to put their own needs (ego, career development, recognition, etc.) ahead of the collective goals of the team when individuals aren't held accountable. If a team has lost sight of the need for achievement, the business ultimately suffers.

The Rewards

Striving to create a functional, cohesive team is one of the few remaining competitive advantages available to any organization looking for a powerful point of differentiation. Functional teams avoid wasting time talking about the wrong issues and revisiting the same topics over and over again because of lack of buy-in. Functional teams also make higher quality decisions and accomplish more in less time and with less distraction and frustration. Additionally, "A" players rarely leave organizations where they are part of a cohesive team.

Successful teamwork is not about mastering subtle, sophisticated theories, but rather about embracing common sense with uncommon levels of discipline and persistence. Ironically, teams succeed because they are exceedingly human. By acknowledging the imperfections of their humanity, members of functional teams overcome the natural tendencies that make teamwork so elusive.

The Five Dysfunctions of a Team & The Role of the Team Leader

#1: Absence of Trust - The fear of being vulnerable with team members prevents the building of trust within the team.

#2: Fear of Conflict - The desire to preserve artificial harmony stifles the occurrence of productive, ideological conflict.

#3: Lack of Commitment - The lack of clarity or buy-in prevents team members from making decisions they will stick to.

#4: Avoidance of Accountability - The need to avoid interpersonal discomfort prevents team members from holding one another accountable for their behaviors and performance.

#5: Inattention to Results: The pursuit of individual goals and personal status erodes the focus on collective success.

NONE OF US
IS AS SMART
AS ALL OF US.

DR. KEN BLANCHARD,
CO-AUTHOR OF THE
ONE MINUTE MANAGER

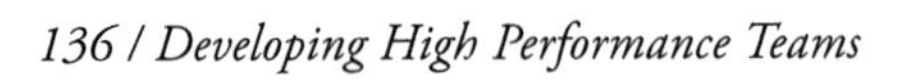

ACKNOWLEDGEMENTS

I am grateful to my clients and past participants for their creative ideas and suggestions, many of which are included in this book. In particular, I would like to thank the following organizations for their support of our team development activities:

- Alcoa
- American Petroleum Institute
- Apache Corporation
- Aramco
- Baylor College of Medicine
- BP
- Calpine
- Chase Bank
- Coca-Cola
- Dow
- El Paso Corporation
- ExxonMobil
- Ford
- Harris County, Texas
- Hunt Oil
- IBM
- KBR
- Lockheed-Martin
- Marathon EG LNG
- NASA
- Occidental Petroleum
- P T Arun LNG
- P T Badak LNG
- Pennzoil
- Schlumberger
- Shell
- Suburban Propane
- Sunoco
- United Technologies
- Wood Group

I extend special thanks to my colleagues, Dianne Bobko, Barbara Dressler, Debbie Sprague, and Barbara Gorman for their outstanding support at North American Training and Development, Inc. I appreciate their contributions to the success of our team building programs and the first edition of this book. I also thank Trisha Keel of Tomorrow's Key for her invaluable contributions in the editing, graphic design, and layout for both editions of this book.

I am especially grateful for the love and support of my wife Mona and my entire family. Their constant encouragement and flexibility have made my life and my work a joy!

Over the past 40 years I have had the privilege to work with and learn from many extraordinary colleagues and clients. I would like to acknowledge my most memorable mentors and supporters:

Ohio University – During my MBA Program at Ohio University, I worked as the Graduate Assistant for two exceptionally talented professors: Dr. Paul Hersey and Dr. Ken Blanchard. Their famous concept of "Situational Leadership" was in its early stage of development at that time. Paul and Ken have become my lifelong friends and colleagues.

University of Houston – Shortly after beginning my Ph.D. Program at the University of Houston, Dr. "Dutch" Holland hired me as a research scientist in the Center for Management Studies and Analysis (CEMSA) at NASA's Johnson Space Center. That opportunity allowed me to work in one of the most exciting organizations in the world and establish a 40-year relationship with JSC.

NASA–Johnson Space Center – There are hundreds of people who have supported my work with JSC. The most notable are Frank Benz, Mike Coats, Aaron Cohen, Allen Flynt, Gerry Griffin, Wayne Hale, Harv Hartman, Greg Hayes, Paul Hill, Tommy Holloway, Jeff Howell, Carolyn Huntoon, Chris Kraft, Gene Kranz, Lucy Kranz, Mike Kincaid, Jack Lister, Glynn Lunney, Leonard Nicholson, Ellen Ochoa, Henry Pohl, Brady Pyle, Natalie Saiz, Melanie Saunders, Eileen Stansbery, Randy Stone, Dot Swanson, Joel Walker, and Philip Whitbeck. I would also like to express my gratitude to my program coordinators who have made my work with Johnson Space Center so enjoyable and effective: Tommy Capps, John Duncan, Diane DeTroye, Greg Grant, Diane Kutchinski, Erica Vandersand, Susan White, and Patt Williams.

ExxonMobil – Since 1980, many people within ExxonMobil have provided opportunities for me and NATD. In particular I would like to acknowledge the support of Neil Blackburn, Randy Broiles, Jim Broussard, Paul Caldwell, Guy Cook, Don Cooper, Neil Cowley, Alex Guiscardo, Norm Hill, Udom Inoyo, Bruce Jones, Alfred Koch, Wally Luthy, Jim Massey, Jay Medley, Cyril Odu, Solomon Oladunni, and Mark Ward.

BP – In the 1980s, I was conducting leadership and team development programs for Standard Oil Production Company (Sohio). In 1987 BP acquired Sohio, establishing it as the cornerstone of BP America. The new Chief Executive Officer, John Browne, became interested in my training and development programs. Over the next decade, Lord Browne's on-going support provided North American Training and Development with opportunities to work with BP in many locations around the world.

University of Chicago, Booth School of Business – For the past several years I have been invited by Associate Dean Steve La Civita to team-teach the "Situational Leadership" course in the University of Chicago's EMBA Program. I am grateful for the opportunity to collaborate with Dr. Paul Hersey, Dr. Marshall Goldsmith, and Dr. Ron Campbell to present our course at this prestigious school of business.

Authors of Recommended Readings – I also extend my appreciation to authors Jon Katzenbach, Douglas Smith, Pat MacMillan, and Patrick Lencioni and their publishers for permission to reproduce excerpts from their best-selling books on teams in the *Recommended Readings* section of this book.

SERVICES AVAILABLE

Dr. Walt Natemeyer and his colleagues conduct highly successful team development programs throughout the world. Their expert facilitation skills will assure that your Strategic Planning and Team Building efforts are maximized.

For more information about ***Developing High Performance Teams*** or other workshops and consulting services, please contact:

North American Training and Development, Inc.
17041 El Camino Real, Suite 103
Houston, Texas 77058
USA
Phone (281) 488-7000
Fax (281) 488-7088
www.natraining.com

Made in the USA
Charleston, SC
27 January 2012